Ephemera

Ephemera

Evana Bodiker

Texas Review Press
Huntsville, Texas

FIRST EDITION

Requests for permission to acknowledge material from the work should be sent to:

Permissions
Texas Review Press
English Department
Sam Houston State University
Huntsville, TX 77341-2146

The epigraph comes from Susan L. Mitchell's poem "Exile."

"Blue Morpho" was the recipient of second place in the 2017 Anthony Abbott Poetry Contest.

"Pas de deux" received an honorable mention in the 2017 A.R. Ammons Poetry Contest.

"Gas Station Entomology" appeared in its original form in the July 2016 issue of *Vagabond City Literary Journal* as "Gas Station Entomology for a Dragonfly."

"Ode for Uncooked Chicken" was modeled after Sharon Olds' collection *Odes*.

"Ode for Hayes" was modeled after Sylvia Plath's "Ode for Ted" from *The Collected Poems*.

Cover design by Nancy Parsons, www.graphicdesigngroup.net

Library of Congress Cataloging-in-Publication Data

Names: Bodiker, Evana, 1995- author.
Title: Ephemera / Evana Bodiker.
Description: First edition. | Huntsville, Texas : Texas Review Press, [2018]
| Includes bibliographical references.
Identifiers: LCCN 2018002042 | ISBN 9781680031485 (pbk.)
Subjects: LCSH: Chronic diseases--Psychological aspects--Poetry. |
Transitional objects (Psychology)--Poetry
Classification: LCC PS3602.O325655 A6 2018 | DDC 811/.6--dc23 LC record available
at https://lccn.loc.gov/2018002042

For Erica and for Hayes.

Contents

"My wild will spreads its wings and flies."

—Susan L. Mitchell

I.

Fever Ghazal

My skin's temperature announces 103. A fever:
a spiking, sinking, cold sweating fever.

I wish I had a damp washcloth for my forehead.
I beg for respite, but it loves me, this fever.

Once in childlike haze, crying out for Mother,
Grandmother's ghost appeared to me in fever.

Aching, from desert to tundra, there's no other
choice than to stay anchored to this fever.

Red-striped, strep throat, summer aches;
away from home at camp, scarlet in my fever.

Like a melting ice cube, the moon's touch snakes
down my skin; even she can't stop my fever.

Decades of fighting febrility in my bed;
haven't I earned forgiveness from such fever?

Finally, a cool hand touches my forehead.
She blesses, "Little warrior, you'll break this fever."

Ephemera

A peculiar hollowness hovers over the morning—
the crickets rise to greet her heavy steps in the grass.
She savors their love song, but her work does not mourn
their eventual silence. Motionless behind dogwood trees,
hidden for a moment: never happier than when the net
falls in a slow heap over golden bright swallowtail wings.
A simple pinch of thoraxes between thumb and index:
in one squeeze, this benevolent execution
adds to the closemouthed chorus of her collection

displayed in glass frames hung on sky blue walls,
her sunlit prize hall of eternity: cold and still
as a morgue. The crickets' tune hushes to a dirge.
Lightning bugs dodge her, giving away their hiding places.
This Eden is hers. She likes to play God
like God likes to play entomologist with her.

Mold

On the old shower curtain, it grows like ivy
speckled and untrimmed, about to flower.
Scrubbing eradicates the stubborn spots;
bleach fumes build a fortress around me
as my hands delight in this homely task.

I can manage this. I can make this clean;
though of what, I'm unsure. Running my hand
behind the curtain, my fingers flutter
like a cabbage white butterfly's dull wings.
The bleach has fouled me, burning my nostrils,
my bare skin turning whiter than the basin.

When I stand, black dots swarm overhead.
I'm clean though spores linger in my airways.

Swimming Lesson

God goes swimming in the Toe River
      to teach me how to do the butterfly stroke.
I tell him, *Lord, freshwater has never done*
      much for my lungs, to which he replies,
"It isn't about getting worse but staying better."
      Swimming he calls baptism; to learn is to go under,
to be cleansed is to get a nose full of water,
      though I paddle to avoid submersion.
My technique does not improve but he promises
      we can float into the ether of hosanna
and holy mist. The current says I am his chosen one,
      a disciple of exception. I'll wade into an eddy
until the river clears of mud and my insides
      become childlike again.

Fearfully Made

He knows about brain-swelling amoeba,
organ-scarring diseases, pseudomonas summers;
he made them all, not quite his own image
in the cloudiness of my lungs and scarred stomach.
I might call him for replacement, a silver coined bargain,
just five minutes more, a confessional phone conversation.
My soul and body do not consent to each other.
This malady did not bloom overnight. No marigold,
it takes its time to germinate in its soil
and when morning comes with no returned calls,
I'll begin to understand why ragdolls are made.

Nebulizer

Like a deer to a salt lick, I arrive every morning:
vapor brines my mouth and clears the parts
mere inhalation can't reach. The small box's
mouthpiece hums against clenched teeth.
The frantic hive of my lungs is lulled into restless
slumber, their bacteria stilled for a moment.

I return cotton-mouthed to the hazy oracle
before bed, eager for its saline oasis.
As this apothecary machine directs our ritual,
my coughs expel mucus from my chest,
hollowing me out. Even when I dread this routine,
tomorrow, again, I will do, I will do, and I will do.

Gas Station Entomology

Off Interstate-77, she lies
on the pavement: belly up, bulging
eyes to the exhaust-filled, periwinkle
evening sky. This is her deathbed,
a ground covered in a ROYGBIV
of gum, pressed permanently into
the sidewalk by the footfalls of kids
on their way back to their magic carpets
that take them safely to Disney World.
These feet and their popsicle-sticky fingers
did not touch her, to my surprise. She is alone,

safe—her body does not twitch. She
is not surrounded by shocked witnesses
or chalk outlines. Her wings: intact, moving
only slightly with the passing cars' wind.
One week ago, I watched a BBC documentary
on her kind, on the life
she sacrificed to give birth in a dangerous
world. Half awake, I heard the narrator's voice say,
"Her wings are truly tested. If she doesn't
break through the water's surface,
she will drown." The nearest bodies
of water to us now are the Gulf, seventy
miles west, and a pool of spilt soda
a few feet from my sneakers. Her eggs
are not here. The volume was too loud,
causing my sleeping boyfriend
to stir. As I lowered the TV's sound,
I heard him say, "Her success
depends on these fragile wings."

I kneel down and pick her up outside
the Circle K. My sister tells me
not to touch dead things.

II.

Mise En Place

Father, my sliced thumb pleases me.
You are not here to watch me bleed,
to hover over me as I prepare to make

the soup you make better.
I run the cut finger under the tap,
the faint sting of onions sterilizing

the wound, its blood offering
sanctifying my graceless kitchen.
You might stop cooking if cut,

but no small injury will stop
my earnest, haphazard chopping
of the celery, carrots, and over-boiled

chicken. These missteps might cause
you, the patron saint of preparation, to fret.
How many ways have I failed to invoke you?

I praise only myself, an idolatress
of oversalted stock and unevenly
sliced vegetables. My method is

savoring, severing; learned like
a child's eager hand to the hot stove.

Ode to Undercooked Chicken

After Sharon Olds

Cooking has no science,
but instead art, though exactness
sneaks up on creativity, fine seasoning
fails to outwit safety and salmonella.
The garlic burns on the top of the baking
chicken—my substitute for a thermometer,
the rosemary for remembrance of 160 degrees.
Damn this singed old oven mitt and impatience,
these forgiving eyes without glasses that help pass
the chicken's exterior to be as pale as the outside
of my breast, not instead the shy, but quite rosy,
bloom of the areola. I am hungry.
The dim overhang of the kitchen fixture is confirmation
of cooked enough, each bite a nauseating buffet
in the swaying rowboat of my stomach, too soft, too rare,
an imagined feverish call in the night to help expel
the poison I baked, at three hundred degrees,
with onion and lemons and thyme.

Fibrosis

I know it well, sister said, the fine hell
of bluing veins and white, white sheets

marked scarlet by my own hand.
It is a dissatisfied chorus, an unkindness

of ravens beckoning the deed to be done
and for me to do it and do it well.

Over time, more scarring, like yours;
fine as Lichtenberg figures etching me

wrist to elbow and you, lungs
to pancreas. Thick and rigid,

shame filled, blood shod woman,
I carry the press of four years' worth

of quiet knives on my wrists. You hold
in your belly and chest two worn decades,

on the way to ascension, broken down
tissue in every organ except your flesh.

It's what you fear, and what I want;
cruelty in our fates' arrangements,

a carousel of trying to get on death's horse
as you stand in line for discounted time.

My skin exposes me and yours
holds it all in; I am terrified of what

eats you at night, but not of what
marks itself on me. I've let you go,

I've let you go. It's all I can do.
Little sister, your invisible disfigurement emancipates me.

These are my faults, moonlit and obvious,
that kill, that kill—they kill me.

Wasp Nest

They used to come in droves. The wasps
    make their homes in door frames.
I shudder in memoriam of all the ground
    nests he dumped gasoline into,
those sunken sanctuaries, no bother
    to the world above. He fashioned the yard to
a night sky and the nests were unlit Roman candles.
    But only pretend fire, just delight in suffocation,
and the humid closeness of promise to drop
    a match, one sting from total extermination.
I watched from the window, pacing like a widow.

My body doused in his petroleum sweat
    on evenings when he tired of killing
the yellowjackets and needed new land
    to raze. His own sting penetrated my skin,
causing the flesh to swell and when he slept,
    I prayed that God might cover me in
baking soda to draw out the paralyzing poison.
    The neighbors now use humane pesticide.
I walk into spring, praising their nests and
    this time last year when I finally soaked his hive
in gas and never turned to a salt stone, never turned back.

Pas de deux

Mother paints daughter's lips fuchsia
while red matte blots her own front
incisors. They rush, late, for final dress
rehearsal. Her small double complains

about the tulle scratching her foalish
thighs, only moments ago spinning
half-naked in her ballet shoes. Mother
knows there is no future here: struck

by hunger, Daughter begs for fast food
on the way to dance class, her impish
fingers drawing stars on the backseat
window. She tends to give in, but worries

Daughter will know how long bulimia's
aftertaste lingers one day. For now, the little
one hums off-key her recital tune, picking
at the runs in her constricting, pink tights.

She likes the way pirouettes
lift her into the air, weightless. She
sometimes admires herself in the studio
mirror, strutting with duck-like grace.

She does not need to know her legs
will never mimic the disproportionate
doll she leaves, frozen in mid-jeté,
on the car seat when Mother pulls away.

Hess Road Oak

Lightning split the old oak's
sternum, recast it into sapphire
crystal. The tree lay spiteful

on the crown of our ten
acres for years before
murmurs rose to resurrect

it in our minds. Father
mulled over when to haul
the tree off the property,

fearing the weight of its
tonnage. He waited to tear
down its companion barn,

hesitant to build upon any
burial ground he couldn't trace.
We watched from the porch

as he idly mined away,
quarrying the wreckage:
all those branches

once adorned with our lost
toys, that same canopy
we hid under during rain safaris.

Never were we given the chance
to carve lovers' letters or tell
it we love it. Awe traps us under

the oak's branching arms,
stonesetting shadows into our
dreams, long oracle nights,

while he takes another
generation to decide what
to do with its monolithic trunk.

Morning Feeding

Agonized, like a baby bird screeching
for its mother to deliver it an earthworm,
the toddler's hunger sounds set the nursery
going, warned a sleeping house that the time's
arrived for yet another fruitless meal.

Mother Sisyphus climbed the stairs,
nesting the milk bottle between hands
to warm it, hoping it would start the day
with her colic child pacified.

She broke the enzyme capsules in half,
spilling their beads onto the child's tongue.
Then waiting for sobs to turn to suckling,
for her daughter's stomach to announce
with gurgling consent, its wordless gratitude

for her. In the wicker chair, rocking for hours,
she keeps the bottle firm between forming teeth,
the ones she hopes her daughter will soon
learn to use, to chew and to not starve.

III.

Maintenant

I know how I want your days:
all of them. The bedding light
mornings, smothering sheets,
the secret sounds of lip-to-lip,
toe-to-toe, closing the blinds
to exile the rest of the world
from our warm counterpane.
And then breakfast at the restaurant
at the bottom of my hilly street.
In one hand, coffee number six,
the other giving me a cup of iced tea,
half-sweet-half-unsweet, light ice.
These days we now share:
cream cheese on your nose
on a train from London to Henley
or displaced during a movie
because the way our neighbors
chew their popcorn and whisper
makes us want to move seats.
Better at home, bleary-eyed.
Friday afternoon cross-worded
and heavy-browed,
warm February, puzzling
over twenty-seven across,
absent in your mindfulness
of oughts and shoulds;
it's so good not to worry.
As sun drenched and marbled
skin, summer worn and uncertain
of winter but so fine here right now.
Burned on our feet and back
to bed, another day to rest.
Maybe the stars will put

a bag over my head, taking
me away from your everyday,
maybe you'll metamorphose
into a kite without a string.
In my bones, my mind, the loss
of you tingles; on my skin,
for now, you promise tomorrow.

Leah, Late March

In newly elongated evening light,
she sautés onions and peppers on the stove
in her towel. Both our heads are wet, shower-
fresh, and everything is red and yellow.

We catch up as I cleave the broccoli. Over
the next half hour, she stands barefooted
on the peeling linoleum, big toe fiddling
with a hole in the floor, an almost fret,

but she's carefree and laughs at NPR
and never cares how poorly I chop
the florets. I stand close enough
to know a bastion when I see one.

She held my hair the night before,
combing through it in the morning,
to erase the mess she so easily cleaned,
forgiving my faults with her sunlit hands.

I'll remember the blue-washed floor
of the kitchen, the wine bottles plugged
up with melted candles, walking into
the house glorified in its thrift.

She'll leave the stove on when she showers,
but it will all stay the same even after we leave.
The porch's fairy lights flicker as I drive home,
morning dulling the lighthouse's beam.

Blue Morpho

The greenhouse humidity
moved down our backs
like the sweat beads
on our Pimm's cups
hours before in the garden
bar. She was our tiny
liaison, so that he and I
might say the right words
that evening more easily,
a tender empress fluttering
overhead until she chose
to land on his university
sweater first. Her frayed
wings burned cobalt
in the late London
afternoon. She let me
touch her next, climbing
onto my fingers
like they were sugar,
her gentle trapeze
teasing my skin.
He misread her name
on the placard, *morphe*,
but later he christened
her accurately: *morpho*.
For the rest of the day,
I dreamed of her
on my slouched shoulder,
my body an accomplice
in her disappearing act.

Aubade

In the gray held hush of morning,
our bellies become our curving backs

as you become me and I you,
not two but as one in the white

noise rustle of warm, second-skin
sheets. What luck we share,

to wake at the same moment,
a wordless vernacular of yawns

and eyelash kisses. If we were
butterflies, what kind would we be?

Or mourning doves cooing
yes, please stay in bed, no telling

one from the other, one body
splitting one pillow's realty. Close

but never quite enough, stretching
our damp, new wings.

Odysseus

Difficult to divine how you arrived,
not water-doused or mail-slotted to me,
but whole in your stone-centered gaze, almost
tired out by your ninety days under stars.
Satisfied by none, you chose me to be
your canary, waiting, green with hope for

your return. Coming home from the back-woods,
you made me into your mooring, fashioned
yourself into a pilgrim to my bed's
unmade shrine. I'll make a Ulysses out
of you yet. Yes, the butterfly kind, blue
body mild as the Aegean, crushing.

I will weave our dreams together: never
go back to sea without me as your mate.

Commonwealth

White housed hills, the specter
of Jefferson close behind
my lifting legs. My home
scenery bores me,
the cherry blossoms
of this one make me dream.

I can fit here, I say to myself,
running with the fit girls
and boys who live their afternoons
drenched in mimosas, free
in their founding father's gaze
to drink and to breathe.

Out of air, it's so colonial
and I'm taking big spoonfuls
of it, my lungs swelling
like fresh peaches one bite
from bursting. We round
one more corner, all splendor.

I'm in no hurry to outrun
the others. On sun-drenched streets,
ash trees stand tall as guards
and I want to lose myself
in the esoteric tradition
of wealth, comfort, intellect.

The octagons beckon me
into their column arms;
to disappear now into the anciently
designed wonders might spoil the run,
but I'd shed my shoes in a wink
to lie serpentine in this grass forever.

We sprint towards the race's
end and my mind buzzes again,
back to the world I come from,
of a countryside drive home,
sunburnt in the passenger seat,
checking the rearview every so often.

Ode for Hayes

After "Ode for Ted" by Sylvia Plath

Under my man's watchful eye,
bobwhites flit; he calls
them family. He knows why the crows
gather most mornings
on the garage roof, not a warning
but a boon in the floodlight's glow.

Boxwood hedges, he says, stand
enchanted by mother's hand,
a magic ring
on the proud front lawn,
his destiny drawn
in an oracle magnolia spring.

For his next spell, he takes
me to the silver lake
moonlight casts on the kitchen floor—
the linoleum shining rarely,
his childhood visions carrying me early
into morning, the larks at his door.

Mockingbirds rest well in his wood,
and I could too, always, for good.
How glad I'd be not to know
all the things I shouldn't read
but like Adam's woman, I need
him wandering constantly in my wood.

Pollen Season

How odd to like the way pollen
stains the streets neon after the rain
like a birthday party cleared out
before I opened my dry eyes.
Even though the way my throat
swells at the sight of the choleric
puddles, or how I can barely breathe
at all this time of year, it's nice

when the garish gold grows happy
inside me. How I wish it would just
take me upstairs and dye my skin
its color. I won't cry on the bus
today. *Stay alive,* I tell myself
like it's some half-pebbled promise
or a repeating truth about flowers
in May following April rain.

My hands imprint all I touch:
a chalk outline of personhood
on car doors, the empty mailbox—
until a thunderstorm comes
to wash away the latent dusting.
I want a lasting veil of yellow,
for someone to realize, before the pollen
covers the world again, that I was here.

Acknowledgements

This chapbook would not have been possible without the guidance and instruction of Michael McFee at the University of North Carolina at Chapel Hill.

To my mother and father for giving me life and love and laughter and the belief in myself to write. For believing in me. I love you both.

To Erica my first editor, my first friend, my first love, my forever soul mate.

To Rain Tiller, Emma Holcomb, Leah Balkoski, Lindsay Macchio, Gaby Nair, Gavin Phillips, Elizabeth Beckman, Caby Styers, Taylor Cannon, and Lily Stephens for showing me real love and nurturing me and crying with me and growing with me.

To Ross White who told me I was indeed a poet, and who shaped my first poems when they were just balls of clay.

To Gabrielle Calvocoressi the professor and guide of my poetics after these poems were written, but someone who has been there all along.

To Salem Dockery and Paul Smith for reading endless drafts of poems and always saying yes to writing more, more, more.

To Hayes Cooper for everything, for always, for us.

CPSIA information can be obtained
at www.ICGtesting.com
Printed in the USA
BVHW03s0442100418
512890BV00010B/27/P